THE
GOOD
AND
ANCIENT
WAY

CHRISTIAN SPIRITUALITY
FOR POST-MODERN TIMES

RAY SIKES

ISBN: 1482024349
ISBN-13: 9781482024340

Cover and book design by Levi Dylan Sikes

Contents

I | How to Read This Book

Thus says the Lord: "Stand by the roads, and look, and ask for the ancient paths, where the good way is; and walk in it, and find rest for your souls."

Jeremiah 6:16

This brief book was written to help people develop a deep and abundant life with God. Its ideas are not new, nor are they uniquely creative, and what follows consists of little more than summaries and paraphrases of the Bible itself. In fact, the usual conventions for using quoted material have been exceeded, and a fair amount of the text is nothing other than Scripture itself because those timeless words have transformed more lives than any other.

Therefore, read carefully, asking God to give you insight, and remain open to what he will show you. At times his revelations will be shocking and discomforting, but if you continue in God's word, "you will know the truth, and the truth will set you free" (John 8:32). You may want to read this book in its entirety, simply going from cover to cover, but eventually find a good translation of the Bible and delve into the Scriptures for yourself. Quotations in this book are from the English Standard Version, and it is available at no cost online or may be purchased inexpensively in stores. The same is also true of many other translations.

Look up the portions of Scripture listed at the end of each section of this book, as these verses are the basis for the ideas found in the text. Of course, you may want to also look up the parenthetical references, too, so that you can see the quoted or paraphrased passages in their original context. Read the Bible even more slowly and carefully than you might read the book you now hold, for it will vanish and be forgotten, but as long as there is a world with people, the Bible will endure.

Some verses are referenced multiple times in this book, but you should not hesitate to read these passages over and over again, because there is always some new challenge, comfort, or insight to encounter, even in familiar portions of the Bible. Let these discoveries spur you on in praying honestly and without religious pretensions to God himself. Through all these efforts make it your goal to know God more deeply and to do his will more completely.

II | The Way of Scripture

Before it was called Christianity, the biblical book of Acts records that the religion was considered a sect and called The Way. This was not a mere doctrine or creed, nor was it a program or academic course of study. Prior to the church becoming a massive worldwide institution with seemingly countless denominations, theologies, and traditions, the faith was a simple way of life revolving around the person of Jesus Christ, who actually referred to himself as "the way, and the truth, and the life" (John 14:6).

The essence of this spirituality has been preserved for thousands of years in the Bible, a collection of writings that has admittedly been quoted, misquoted, and used to legitimize and promote causes and agendas that actually have little to do with what is really in the Scriptures. Even the sacred writings of other religions have heavily borrowed from its words, and the very fact that the Bible has been used and misused so widely only reaffirms its inherent truth, beauty, and power.

Many non-biblical writings indeed reveal aspects of life and truth because God is the ultimate source of anything that has value: "Do not be deceived, my beloved brothers. Every good gift and every perfect gift is from above, coming down from the Father of lights with whom there is no variation or shadow due to change"(James 1:17).

The Bible is unique, however, in that it is a collection of diverse literary forms, written by scores of authors over more than a thousand years. It has been tested and recognized by godly people through the ages, who have regarded the Bible as peculiarly given by God himself. These ancient writings were "breathed out by God"(II Tim 3:16) through authors inspired by the Holy Spirit. Consequently, the text they wrote has been reverently preserved and carefully translated into more languages than any other literary work. We all would do well to read these words for ourselves and let them affect our lives as no other book can or should.

Scripture, unlike other writings, is a "living and active" document that can examine us more than we scrutinize it, "piercing to the division of soul and spirit and discerning the thoughts and intentions of the heart" (Heb 4:12). Before we can know God, we must be honest with ourselves, but who can truly know himself or herself? We deceive ourselves into thinking we are either more or less than we are, and we are quick to shift blame for our shortcomings, but the Word of God has the power to cut through our layers of self-deception. When we allow the Word of God to do its proper work within our hearts and minds, it produces a life of eternal value, for "all flesh is like grass…The grass withers, and the flower falls, but the word of the Lord remains forever" (I Peter 1:24-25).

The Word of God is like seed sown in the soil of our hearts, which leads to spiritual life and growth. His word also functions as a light in the darkness, giving enough illumination for us to get our bearings and move through life without stumbling over that which we cannot perceive. The Bible does not contain the answer to every question we might have, and much is left shrouded in mystery, despite theologians' vain attempts to nail down virtually every detail about God and his dealings with humans. Questions about destiny and freewill, good and evil, justice and injustice, and many other quandaries will continue plaguing our minds and squelching our hope and faith if we let them. Even if we spend our lifetimes delving into the holy writings, we will probably be more aware of the vastness of what we do not know than when we first started, but enough is given merely in the Gospel of John that we may know "Jesus is the

Christ, the Son of God" and "have life in his name" (John 20:31). In that life he gives us, we find confidence in God so that we may love, trust, and obey him in spite of our questions.

Scriptures for Reflection and Prayer

—

Psalm 119:89-112
2 Timothy 3:14-17
2 Peter 1: 19-21
2 Peter 3: 15-18

III | The Wisdom of God and the Wisdom of the World

The knowledge of God and his ways comes from him and not ourselves, but for us to recognize the power and authority of his message, we must be open to doing the will of God. Most of us, in all our questioning and skepticism, really don't want to know the truth, because we inherently know that if there is a God, we owe him our very lives. Consequently, we may approach God not with honest questions, but with excuses for unbelief, allowing us to continue along our own way.

Many doubted Jesus and his teachings, but he gave the prerequisite for recognizing the truth when we find it: "If anyone's will is to do God's will, he will know whether the teaching is from God or if I am speaking on my own authority" (John 7:17). Quite simply, most of us are not willing to do what God desires for us, and therefore we remain unenlightened. If we cling to our own ideas and arrogantly assume we can go on living as we always have, or that we can reason our way to a form of redemption on our own terms, we will miss the revelation of God. In the New Testament writings, certain Greeks and Jews represent forms of knowledge that suppress the truth, and these ways of thinking persist to this present day.

The Greeks were founders of what has become modern philosophy and science. While their contributions have led to many advances, these disciplines have limited value in spiritual matters and can actually hinder us when cultivating a relationship with God or living a life worthy of his glory. For example, the scientific method allows us to examine phenomena in the natural world and draw reasonable conclusions, but it cannot accommodate a God who transcends what may be observed and tested. Scientists have concluded that the universe has not always existed, but had a definite beginning in time, commonly referred to as "the big bang." Those with faith, however, have acknowledged the more essential truth since ancient times: "In the beginning, God created the heavens and earth" (Genesis 1:1). While the Bible provides a creation account that does not satisfy scientific skeptics, believers have embraced those words as either a metaphoric or utterly supernatural explanation pointing to realities beyond our own limited comprehension. In like manner, humanity's collective intellect and impressive tools of observation have exponentially increased our knowledge, reducing the building blocks of the galaxies to subatomic particles as scientists seek to explain how mass itself exists; however, for thousands of years believers have recognized that God "is before all things and in him all things hold together" (Colossians 1:17).

Beyond and above scientific knowledge is a God who cannot be truly known through mere intellect. Real faith has its origins in God himself, and it is not just a reasoned conclusion based on evidence. It is also more tangible than simple mental agreement with particular ideas because "faith is the assurance of things hoped for, the conviction of things not seen. For by it, the people of old received their commendation. By faith we understand that the universe was created by the word of God, so that what is seen was not made out of things that are visible" (Heb 11:1-3).

A lack of this very real faith also beset many of the Jewish leaders in New Testament times. Some demanded supernatural signs before they would believe in Christ. Of course, the biblical record reveals time and time again that even when provided with miracles, people still persist in unbelief. Exodus records that Moses led the people of Israel through the desert, yet God was not pleased with the vast majority of them, for they lacked faith despite physical manifestations from God in the form of pillars of cloud and fire, supernatural provision of food and water, and deliverance from the pursuing army of Egypt.

Besides asking for supernatural signs when none were needed, some unbelieving Jews held to a religion full of traditions that were actually unscriptural and devoid of spiritual life. Jesus quoted the prophet Isaiah in reference to their hypocrisy: "This people honors me with their lips, but their heart is far from me; in vain do they worship me, teaching as doctrines the commandments of men" (Matthew 15:8-9). Similar forms of dead religion are also found among far too many professing Christians who are judgmental and legalistic, demonstrating "bitter jealousy and selfish ambition" instead of living according to the godly wisdom that is "peaceable, gentle, open to reason, full of mercy and good fruits" (James 3:14, 17).

Through the world's philosophies, modern science, and even many religious traditions, we will not find the revelation of God, because "the wisdom of this world is folly with God" (1 Corinthians 3:19). Then, how do we begin to actually make progress on this way of faith? We must approach God with humility and a sense of need, and not be like those who attempt to study him and demand answers to all of their questions, many of which are quite unanswerable in the first place, for his judgments and actions in history are far beyond human comprehension.

Theologians have debated various issues down through the centuries and held to speculative conclusions that have been defended, at times even at the cost of human lives, because dead and worldly religion demands certainties. Those with God-given faith, however, are able to leave certain mysteries to God. It is somewhat ironic that one section of Scripture that has been the source for many theological debates ends with these words: "Oh, the depth of the riches and wisdom and knowledge of God! How unsearchable are his judgments and how inscrutable are his ways! 'For who has known the mind of the Lord, or who has been his counselor? Or who has given a gift to him that he might be repaid?' For from him and through him and to him are all things. To him be the glory forever"(Romans 11:33-36). It seems that good theology should lead to a final point of worship and trust in God, who by his very nature transcends our own understanding, rather than breeding ceaseless speculations.

Jesus proclaimed that God has "hidden these things from the wise and understanding and revealed them to little children" (Matt 11:25), and "whoever does not receive the kingdom of God like a child shall not enter it" (Luke 18:17). Therefore, we must approach the Scriptures humbly and simply like children in need, acknowledging our lack of ability to fathom the wisdom of God on our own and understanding that "faith comes by hearing and hearing by the word of Christ" (Romans 10:17).

Scriptures for Reflection and Prayer
—
1 Corinthians 1:18-2:16
James 3:13-18

IV | God is Near

The visible universe in its overwhelming depth and breadth points us to an invisible Creator because "the heavens declare the glory of God, and the sky above proclaims his handiwork" (Psalm 19:1). Contrary to what some religions teach, God is not nature itself, for he "has set his glory above the heavens" (Psalm 8:1), and while we live in a universe that consists of physical matter, "God is spirit and those who worship him must worship in spirit and in truth" (John 4:24). All that God created has a beginning, but he does not. He is infinite and dwells outside of time itself because even time is his own fabrication.

Many put aside the obvious revelation of God demonstrated in the earth and sky and instead worship nature itself, or they create gods of their own imagination, or they suppress their awareness of him, even though "his invisible attributes, namely, his eternal power and divine nature, have been clearly perceived, ever since the creation of the world, in the things that have been made" (Romans 1:20). Many pretend that God does not exist, and, supposing the universe to be some sort of cosmic accident, they live as they please apart from their Creator's kind intentions for them.

Consequently, as people seek out lives apart from him, God gives them over to the depravity of their own minds, and they become creators of evil, devising expressions of wickedness that stand contrary to God's purposes. We need not look far to see the arrogance, evil, and perversion of humankind. People lie to one another, steal what is not their own, and spread gossip and slander. They disrespect their own parents, exploit and objectify men and women and even children through unrestrained sexual passion, and murder their own kind. Worse still, in the recesses of their hearts, "though they know God's decree that those who practice such things deserve to die, they not only do them but give approval to those who practice them" (Romans 1:32). Before we nod our heads in agreement and rue the evil of others, we must look within our own selves, realizing that each of us must stand before our Creator and give an account for not only our actions, but for our innermost thoughts as well, because "God judges the secrets of men by Christ Jesus" (Romans 2:16). Therefore, we ought not to judge others; God is the only true judge, and each of us will individually stand or fall before him.

Because awareness persists among people that there is a God, the religious impulse is ever present despite a vast diversity of races and cultures, so that both repression of the knowledge of God and a quest for him are virtually universal. The Apostle Paul recognized these contradictions in our species when he preached in Athens among temples honoring the gods and goddesses of Greek mythology. He perceived that this was a religious people, but made it plain that God does not dwell in temples built by human design and labor, and he needs nothing that we might give him. People were created in such a way that "they should seek God, in the hope that they might feel their way toward him and find him. Yet he is actually not far from each of us" (Acts 17:27). Paul went on and verified some of the truth they had already believed by quoting their own writings about God and his nearness: "In him we live and move and have our being" (Acts 17:28). He continued, though, declaring that God may have previously "overlooked" their ignorance, but "now he commands all people everywhere to repent, because he has fixed a day on which he will judge the world in righteousness" (Acts 17:30-31). For all of us, the message is the same: we must turn away from our own thoughts, desires, and sins, and then turn to God completely.

Scriptures for Reflection and Prayer

—

Acts 17:22-34
Romans 1:16-2:16

V | Jesus, Revealer of God

Jesus called himself the "light of the world," so those who follow him no longer have to grope blindly for God, but rather may be illuminated by Christ (John 8:12). As mere humans, we can only have a partial knowledge of God. Because "our God is a consuming fire" (Hebrews 12:29) and in his pure and holy essence he overwhelms us, he had to devise ways of making himself understood to fallible and sinful people without destroying them.

Through the Old Testament prophets, glimpses of God's grace and glory were revealed, but their writings are often mystifying and difficult to understand. In Christ, however, their words become clearer. In him we can see the glory of God in an understandable expression and enter into a liberty and freedom where we can be transformed into that very same image of holiness. In the succession of recorded history, God spoke "at many times in many ways" through prophets, and he finally spoke to us through the person of Jesus Christ, who is "the radiance of the glory of God

17

and the exact imprint of his nature" (Hebrews 1:1-3). In Jesus, we can see what God is like, for "he is the image of the invisible God" (Colossians. 1:15), and Jesus even said of himself, "Whoever has seen me has seen the Father" (John 14:9).

Jesus always existed in the "form of God" (Philippians 2:6) with the Heavenly Father and the Holy Spirit, possessing the same type and qualities of divinity. This concept of one God—not several or many gods—but one God in three persons, sets Christianity apart from other religions. Granted, such a concept seems paradoxical and even contradictory, but it reveals an incomprehensible and transcendent Lord who exists in perfect fellowship with himself, one who needs nothing and is completely self-fulfilled. Because there are three persons in complete harmony within one God, Scripture can rightly declare, "God is love" (1 John 4:16), for love is never a solitary experience. In a flagrant display of God's love and generosity, he reached out and invited us into this relationship when the second person of this Holy Trinity "did not count equality with God a thing to be grasped, but made himself nothing, taking on the form of a servant, being found in the likeness of men" (Philippians 2:6-7).

God came in the flesh when Jesus was miraculously born to a virgin named Mary and her husband

Joseph. Jesus had enjoyed unbroken fellowship with God the Father and God the Holy Spirit since before his earthly parents' ancestors were even born, and this is why he could say, "Before Abraham was, I am" (John 8:58.). His use of the syntactically awkward phrase "I am" further affirmed Christ's divinity, for this is the name God used when revealing himself to Moses (Exodus 3:14).

God had promised the patriarch Abraham that one would come as a Savior and eventually bless the entire world. The Old Testament prophets also bore witness in multiple ways, proclaiming revelatory glimpses of Jesus and his life here on earth (1 Peter 1:10-11). Hundreds of years later, Christ did come, making his living as a humble carpenter before ministering and "doing good, healing those who were oppressed by the devil" (Acts 10:38) and performing miracles, even raising the dead back to life. He was put to death on a cross, but rose from the dead and appeared to not only his disciples and the women who were close to his ministry, but also to "more than 500 men" (1 Corinthians 15: 3-6), and many of them were still alive and able to testify to the truth of this statement when it was penned by the Apostle Paul.

Still, many did not recognize Jesus because they sought a political reformer, an earthly king who would change the unjust world systems. Instead,

Jesus came to establish a heavenly kingdom not of this world. Rather than coming in judgment and casting down his enemies, he came as a Savoir, one who would begin his revolution by transforming individual persons' hearts, not human institutions. Many never understood who Jesus really was and ignored or rejected him, the same as today, but "to all who did receive him, who believed in his name, he gave the right to become children of God" (John 1:12).

Scriptures for Reflection and Prayer

—

John 1:1-18
2 Corinthians 3:14-4:6
Hebrews 1:1-2:4

VI | Our Response to the Revelation of God in Christ

A simple fisherman, who would later be known as the Apostle Peter, worked all night, but caught nothing. When Jesus told him to go back out into the very same water and let down his nets yet again, his obedience to Christ's words resulted in a supernatural catch of fish that gave Peter a glimpse of Jesus as someone who was much more than a moral and religious teacher. Only later would he truly understand the reality of Christ as God in the flesh and Savior of humanity, but he was nonetheless overwhelmed and said to Jesus, "Depart from me, for I am a sinful man, O Lord" (Luke 5:8).

Peter's response was not unique. Because Jesus is the Light of the World, "everyone who does wicked things hates the light and does not come to the light, lest his works should be exposed" (John 3:20). Like Peter, we may view Jesus from afar and feel relatively good about ourselves. Once we encounter Christ more completely, however, our impulse is to react in denial and disbelief or, like Peter, beg him to leave us alone.

Even still, Jesus compels us to come to him, for he promised that by the Holy Spirit he would "draw all people to himself" (John 12:32). After he was nailed to a cross, died, rose from the grave, and ascended again to heaven, Jesus made a way for a person to come to him fearlessly. This freedom, in coming to the light of God and living in that radiance, in doing the will of God and being released from the bondage of sin, is the freedom Jesus promised when he said, "If you abide in my word, you will know the truth, and the truth will set you free" (John 8:31-32).

Peter eventually was set free because Jesus did not turn his back on him. Instead, Peter left his boat, his nets, his fish, his entire way of life, and he followed Christ. Peter learned his lessons well, and after Jesus departed from this world, his work continued by the Holy Spirit through Peter and others like him who left everything to follow Jesus and carry this message forward: "Repent therefore, and turn again that your sins may be blotted out, that times of refreshing may come from the presence of the Lord" (Acts 3:19-20).

This turning from ourselves and surrendering without reservation to Christ is the only acceptable response to his holiness and favor toward us. We should not think that we can obtain God's blessings and simply go our own way. No, we must submit to him fully, exchanging our life for his. Jesus made it plain that truly believing in him meant an end to life on our own terms when he said, "If anyone would come after me, let him deny himself and take up his cross daily and follow me. For whoever would save his life, will lose it, but whoever loses his life for my sake will save it. For what does it profit a man if he gains the whole world and loses or forfeits himself?" (Luke 9: 23-24)

Scriptures for Reflection and Prayer

—

Luke 5:1-11
John 3:13-21
Acts 3:18-26

VII | The Holiness of God, the Law, and Following Christ

We must not assume that by turning from ourselves to God we simply behave in a new way, and we somehow try to be better people. Such thinking only reveals our ignorance of God's purpose for our lives, and it is an affront to his holiness, for our own efforts to reform ourselves in order to find acceptance with him will ultimately fail. God reveals his standards of behavior in his holy laws, parts of which are expressed in the Ten Commandments. In these we see a condemnation of lying, stealing, adultery, lusting after another's spouse, dishonoring parents, murder, longing for others' possessions, disregarding the Sabbath, and taking God's name in vain.

In the very first commandment God tells us, "You shall have no other gods besides me" (Exodus 20:3). This commandment is further reaching than it seems, for while most of us do not bow down before idols of wood or stone, we do place virtually everything above the Lord in actual practice. Our lifestyles reveal that we are idolaters at heart, doing whatever pleases us, and by our behaviors we distance ourselves from God, thereby denying him and coming under his judgment. For example, if we lie, steal, or sleep with another person's spouse, we are living as if we have a god other than the true God of Righteousness.

Jesus encountered a young man who wanted to know what he had to do in order to have eternal life. When he claimed to have kept all the Ten Commandments ever since he was a boy, Jesus then said to him, "One thing you still lack. Sell all that you have and distribute to the poor and you will have treasure in heaven; and come, follow me" (Luke 18:22). The man was sad and walked away because he was very rich, and Jesus had revealed the man's true god: his possessions. Like many, this man derived his security and identity from what he owned and his station in life, and it may be inferred that he did whatever he wanted with his great wealth.

This desire to live our lives on our own terms violates the two greatest commandments, which according to Jesus are the essence of all of the law and prophets: "You shall love the Lord your God with all your heart and with all your soul and with all your mind. This is the great and first commandment. And the second is like it: You shall love your neighbor as yourself" (Matthew 22:37-39). These commandments, which reflect the true requirements of godliness, are impossible for any of us to fulfill, "for all have sinned and fall short of the glory of God" (Romans 3:23).

Jesus disclosed that on the Day of Judgment some will claim to have done wonderful religious deeds and yet not enter the kingdom of heaven because they did not do as God had wished them to do. They will protest, saying, "Lord, did we not prophesy in your name, and cast out demons in your name, and do many mighty works in your name?" He will answer them, "I never knew you; depart from me, you workers of lawlessness" (Matthew 7:21-23).

Three fatal flaws mark these condemned people's lives. They presumed religious works could earn them favor with God, their lives were characterized by unrighteousness, and most importantly, they were not in relationship with Christ. For all of us, there is this dilemma: how can we be in relationship with this holy God who revealed himself in Jesus, when all of us at heart are sinful idolaters, doing our own will and not God's?

Scriptures for Reflection and Prayer

—

Exodus 20:1-21
Matthew 5:17-48
Luke 18:18-30

VIII | The Purpose of God's Laws and the Remedy for Our Sin

The commandments of God were never meant to bring us into right standing with him, even though they provide wise guidelines for living a good life, and these same laws may form a foundation in society that promotes peace and security by restraining evildoers. While correct behavior may indeed have positive results, "the law is not laid down for the just but for the lawless and disobedient" (1 Timothy 1:9), for the righteous have found their good standing with God by some other means than the impossibility of fulfilling the righteous requirements of a perfect God by imperfectly keeping a set of rules. God's commandments never justified anyone, for through these laws comes an awareness of sin "so that every mouth may be stopped, and the whole world may be held accountable to God. For by works of the law no human being will be justified in his sight, since through the law comes knowledge of sin" (Romans 3:19-20).

Ultimately we are held to God's standards, but too often we seek to justify ourselves through comparisons with others. Those who have found favor with God have stopped measuring themselves by the people around them, assuming they are more righteous than others and are therefore accepted by God. Jesus renounced this way of thinking when he told the story of a religious man who thanked God that he was not like others who were "extortioners, unjust, adulterers or even like this tax collector," referring to the man who was praying beside him. The religious man went on to remind God that he fasted and gave away a tenth of his income. Conversely, the "evil" tax collector, "would not even lift his eyes to heaven, but beat his breast, saying, 'God, be merciful to me, a sinner.'" Jesus explained that the tax collector, not the religious man, "went down to his house justified… for everyone who exalts himself will be humbled, but the one who humbles himself will be exalted" (Luke 18:9-14).

In this world, pride and self-exaltation cause people to compare themselves to others and seek the approval and esteem of those around them, but God will have nothing to do with this charade. When we judge ourselves against others, we forget that we are not excused by their apparent lack of righteousness; instead, we are judged against God's complete holiness. Furthermore, we cannot seek the approval of men and count their esteem as a measure of our own worthiness before God. Jesus told certain religious people of his day, "How can you believe, when you receive glory from one another and do not seek the glory that only comes from God?" (John 5:44)

Similarly, when bad things happen to people, we too often assume they are more wicked than we are and basically are getting what they deserve. Jesus addressed this very issue when he recounted a particular tragedy that was familiar to his listeners. "Those eighteen on whom the tower in Siloam fell and killed them: do you think that they were worse offenders than all the others who lived in Jerusalem? No, I tell you; but unless you repent, you will all likewise perish" (Luke 13:4-5).

God calls all of us to repentance, which implies a turning to God, but between God and ourselves there are always the sinful violations of his holy law that condemn us. Before the time of Christ, the godly people of the Old Testament found favor with God, not through keeping the law, but through faith in the God of the laws, who used the law as "our guardian until Christ came, in order that we might be justified by faith" (Galatians 3:24). Prior to Christ's coming, righteous people offered sacrifices for their sins, trusting that God, not the sacrifices, would cleanse them from their sin through their acts of faith, but they looked ahead to one who would be a Savior. An angel revealed to Joseph that Mary had conceived by the Holy Spirit that promised Redeemer, and he should name the child Jesus because "he will save his people from their sins" (Matthew 1:21). Even Peter, who left everything to follow Jesus, did not at first understand the nature of this great salvation. He and many other Jews of his day assumed a Savior would come and set them free from the oppression of the Romans, but the greater bondage was not one of political systems, but of the sin present in their own hearts.

Jesus came and revealed God to us, but he also made a way to remove our sin so that we may enter into fellowship with him, and he did this by sacrificing himself for humanity's transgressions. His own disciples only understood this after the fact, for when Christ was captured by the political and religious leaders of his day and murdered on a cross, they assumed his mission had failed. Later, they understood that Jesus had died to pay the penalty of our sins, which is eternal death and separation from a holy God who, because of his very nature, can have no fellowship with anything that is tainted by evil.

Only when we see Jesus wrongly accused and found guilty of offenses that he did not commit, do we truly perceive sin's power to warp and pervert justice and truth. We understand sin's far reaching ramifications as we glimpse not only the suffering of Christ, but also the weeping and fear among those who loved him when their leader was led away for execution like a common criminal. Finally, we understand that the sheer horror and repulsiveness of our transgressions was borne in Christ's body, beaten and bloodied and nailed to cross in one of the most insidious and torturous deaths ever devised by wicked men.

The sins of the world and of our very selves were made manifest at the cross of Christ. When the weight and pain and utter vileness of sin was placed upon him, God the Father had to turn away from God the Son, causing Jesus to cry out, "My God, my God, why have you forsaken me?" (Matthew 27:46)

As light and dark simply cannot coexist, so sinful people cannot live forever with a holy God. Jesus solved our dilemma and rescued us by offering himself on the cross, bearing the burden of our transgressions and dying for our sins. His sacrificial act of obedience to the Heavenly Father's will "made us alive together with him, having forgiven our trespasses, by canceling the record of debt that stood against us with its legal demands. This he set aside, nailing it to the cross" (Colossians 2:13-14).

Our sin makes us God's enemies, for it cannot abide with his holiness and purity, yet Jesus made peace with God possible. This salvation, however, is not automatically given to everyone, but must be received through faith.

Scriptures for Reflection and Prayer
—
Matthew 27:11-54
Romans 3:19-4:8
Galatians 3:10-4:7
Hebrews 9:1-28

IX | The Holy Spirit and the New Birth

Jesus rose from the dead, but explained to his disciples that it was better for him to leave and ascend to the right hand of God the Father in heaven, for if he did not go, the Holy Spirit would not be sent. This third person of the Holy Trinity, the Holy Spirit, has now come, revealing both the Father and the Son to the spirits of those who believe, thus fulfilling Christ's promise: "In that day you will know that I am in my Father, and you in me, and I in you" (John 14:20). For this reason, Jesus did not contradict himself when, before ascending to heaven, he told his disciples, "I am with you always, even to the end of the age" (Matthew 28:20). The Holy Spirit actually inhabits the spirits of believers, making the presence of Christ a reality in their lives, bringing to their remembrance the words of Christ, and teaching them in a way that none other can (John 16:12-15).

Amazing as it seems, our own hearts, once the source of our wickedness, can become the dwelling place of God himself. Jesus promised us, "Whoever believes in me, as the Scripture has said, 'Out of his heart will flow rivers of living water'" (John 7: 38). The Apostle Paul considered this a "mystery hidden for ages and generations" but now revealed to those who have "Christ within you, the hope of glory" (Col 1:25-27).

This presence, the very Spirit of the Living God, can be a reality within us, but we must not assume he is already present in our hearts, for apart from God's provision he may be near to us, but never within. Jesus explained, "Unless one is born again, he cannot see the kingdom of God" (John 3:3). This being born from above is the beginning of life in the Spirit, and the passage to this birth is belief, "For God so loved the world that he gave his only Son, that whoever believes in him should not perish, but have eternal life. For God did not send his Son into the world to condemn the world, but in order that the world might be saved through him. Whoever does not believe is condemned already, because he has not believed in the name of the only Son of God" (John 3:16-18).

This belief is not just agreement with certain ideas, but a turning away from our desires, wishes, and vain attempts to justify or excuse ourselves. It is a form of surrender in which we trust and cling to Christ the Savior, who has removed our sin and provided a way to the Heavenly Father. God delights in giving his very Spirit to humble souls in order to rescue them. Jesus gave us a promise when he said, "If you then, who are evil, know how to give good gifts to your children, how much more will the Heavenly Father give the Holy Spirit to those who ask him!" (Luke 11: 13)

Because we trust in the work Jesus accomplished on the cross, thereby breaking down the barrier of sin between us and God, let us cry out to him so that we may be filled with the Spirit of Christ. Then, having in fact received Christ to ourselves, we may begin afresh and anew on God's way of life, not ours.

Scriptures for Reflection and Prayer

—

John 3:1-18
John 14:15-27
John 16: 5-15

X | Works from Faith

Jesus was asked, "What must we do, to be doing the works of God?" He told the people, "This is the work of God, that you believe in him whom he has sent" (John 6:28-29). Before we can do anything of real and eternal value, we must first believe in Christ, and in surrendering to him, we will receive his Spirit within us. Freed at last from the burden and impossibility of attaining right standing with God through keeping the commandments of the Law, we are now able to live life as it ought to be lived, in the liberty of God's grace with the Spirit of Christ guiding us from within. This undeserved favor from God "has appeared, bringing salvation for all people, training us to renounce ungodliness and worldly passions, and to live self-controlled, upright, and godly lives in the present age" (Titus 2:11-12).

We are no longer our own, for "the love of Christ controls us, because we have concluded this: that ... he died for all, that those who live might no longer live for themselves but for him who for their sake died and was raised" (2 Corinthians 5: 14-15). Our belief is never static, and our salvation is not just a release from the penalties of sin. Salvation is much more, and through our works we ought to be creating a life demonstrating God's wholeness, order, and peace. Because we have truly believed, we "work out our own salvation" and this is possible because, by the Spirit, God himself is present within us "both to will and to work for his good pleasure" (Phil 2:12-13).

When we pursue a path of sin and sensuality, our minds become futile in our understanding of morality, and our hearts become dull to the leading of the Spirit. If, on the other hand, we "put on the new self created after the likeness of God" (Ephesians 4:24), we can put aside lies, speak the truth, be in control of our unrighteous anger, and engage in labors that not only provide for our own true needs, but also allow us to share with others. Above all else, we can forgive those who offend us and demonstrate compassion because God in Christ has forgiven us. Because Christ laid down his life for us, we can lay down our lives for others, and in doing so we find the Holy Spirit giving reassurance in our hearts that we are truly children of the living God (1 John 3:16-19).

Our life in God begins within us and allows us to "abstain from sexual immorality; that each one of you know how to control his own body in holiness and honor, not in the passion of lust like the Gentiles who do not know God" (1 Thessalonians 4:3-5). Out of the holiness that he bestows on us in Christ, we can actually begin to fulfill the law by truly loving God and those around us, for God is love, and we have received from him the very love of God in the Spirit (1 John 4:13-16).

This faith we have is not a destination, nor is it a single decision. We cannot walk according to our own wishes and whims and claim we have faith. Our faith is one that results in right living, "For as the body apart from the spirit is dead, so also faith without works is dead" (James 2:26). If we are truly children of God by the new birth of the Spirit, we must stop living lives characterized by sin and instead make a habit of holy behavior. This is because "no one born of God makes a practice of sinning, for God's seed abides in him, and he cannot keep on sinning because he has been born of God. By this it is evident who are the children of God, and who are the children of the devil: whoever does not practice righteousness is not of God, nor is the one who does not love his brother" (I John 3:9-10). Prior to receiving Christ, we were slaves to sin, but once we come to him, we are to be as "slaves to righteousness leading to sanctification" (Romans 6:19), and in all things we must "try to discern what is pleasing to the Lord" (Ephesians 5:10).

We cannot close our eyes to the needs around us, nor should we be overwhelmed by the magnitude of destitution we may encounter. Jesus told us that we could simply offer a drink of water to one of his disciples and have a reward in heaven (Matthew 10:42). In Christ, we find that even the smallest deed done in faith and love has eternal value, but the grander gestures of philanthropy often ring hollow when not done from a heart that is fully his. Jesus once declared that a few coins a poor old widow donated were more valuable to him than the lavish gifts of those who had more money at their disposal, because she had given out of faith and they had not (Luke 21:1-4).

Furthermore, as we grow in the true knowledge of the Lord, we find ourselves becoming "partakers of the divine nature, having escaped the corruption that is in the world because of sinful desire" (2 Peter 1:4). Because of this new temperament we share with God himself, we may complement our "faith with virtue, and virtue with knowledge, and knowledge with self-control, and self-control with steadfastness, and steadfastness with godliness, and godliness with brotherly affection" (2 Peter 1:4-7). As these "qualities" that are from Christ increase in us, we become more and more certain of our calling and right standing before the Lord of all mercies and are more able to do good works resulting from faith in our risen Savior (2 Peter 1:8-12).

Scriptures for Reflection and Prayer
—

Galatians 5:16-24
Ephesians 4:17-32
1 Thessalonians 4:3-12
James 2:14-26
2 Peter 1:2-11
1 John 3:16-24

XI | The Life of Prayer: Part One

Prayer should interweave our Christian lives, and indeed we are exhorted to "pray without ceasing" (1 Thessalonians 5:17). In its truest expression, prayer is simply fellowship with God himself, having as its source the Spirit of God, who is freely given to those who have trusted Christ for their salvation. In fact, apart from the Spirit of God, we are unable to pray rightly: "For we do not know what to pray for as we ought, but the Spirit himself intercedes for us with groaning too deep for words. And he who searches hearts knows what is the mind of the Spirit, because the Spirit intercedes for the saints according to the will of God" (Romans 8: 26-27).

God sets aside the wisdom of men in order to reveal himself and his will, and we cannot effectively pray according to our own thoughts and desires. His is a "secret and hidden wisdom, which God decreed before the ages for our glory" but "these things God has revealed to us through the Spirit." We can trust the Holy Spirit to reveal to us what we need for prayer and all that is really essential in our lives because "the Spirit searches everything, even the depths of God" (1 Corinthians 2:7, 10). He has instructed us, "Be still, and know that I am God" (Psalm 46:10). Out of this stillness, we experience God's presence, and his relationship with us through the Spirit directs our prayers. This same Spirit has always been the source of true prayer and also inspired the biblical writings, which can further instruct us regarding our lifestyle of communion with God.

Commonly referred to as "The Lord's Prayer" and frequently recited by rote in religious gatherings, it is in fact a model for prayer that Jesus gave. It begins, "Our Father in heaven, hallowed be your name" (Matthew 6:9). At its core, true prayer begins with simple worship by focusing on God himself and expressing reverence for him. As his Spirit leads us, we may speak forth words of praise and adoration to God that go far beyond repetition of Christ's words found in his template for prayer.

The next line in Christ's prayer, "Your kingdom come, your will be done, on earth as it is in heaven" (Matthew 6:10), shows us that out of our worship experience, a desire emerges for his kingdom life to be made real in this present world. It is therefore appropriate when we make specific requests for God's divine order to be manifested in our activities, relationships, and spheres of influence, as we pray for his will to be done "on earth as it is in heaven."

"Give us this day our daily bread" (Matthew 6:11) demonstrates that our practical needs can be voiced to God as well, and thus we may pray about our jobs and other material concerns, expecting his loving care in our situations. "Forgive us our sins, for we ourselves forgive everyone who is indebted to us" (Matthew 6:12) reveals the necessity of continually confessing our sins to God and extending that forgiveness to others. "Lead us not into temptation, but deliver us from evil" (Matthew 6:13) indicates that we should request God's wisdom and direction in the details of our lives, which can be laden with distractions, temptations, and snares.

In making private prayer a personal lifestyle, we heed Jesus' exhortation: "When you pray, go into your room and shut the door and pray to your Father who is in secret. And your Father who sees in secret will reward you" (Matthew 6:6). As we draw away to quiet places to be with God alone, we can wait in silence for his guidance in prayer, and then we will make petitions of him that have value instead of muttering long-winded "empty phrases as the Gentiles do, for they think that they will be heard for their many words" (Matthew 6:7).

Because of all Jesus has done in redeeming us to himself and the Heavenly Father, we have free access to him, and we need not even try to impress him with our many words. As Jesus told his disciples, "Until now you have asked for nothing in my name. Ask and you will receive, that your joy may be made full" (John 16:24). In all our prayers that we pray in the name of Jesus, "this is the confidence that we have toward him, that if we ask anything according to his will he hears us. And if we know that he hears us in whatever we ask, we know that we have the requests that we have asked of him" (1 John 5:14-15).

Scriptures for Reflection and Prayer
—
Matthew 6:1-15
John 16:16-28

XII | The Life of Prayer: Part Two

As James wrote, "If any of you lacks wisdom, let him ask God, who gives generously to all without reproach, and it will be given him. But let him ask in faith, with no doubting, for the one who doubts is like a wave of the sea that is driven and tossed by the wind. For that person must not suppose that he will receive anything from the Lord; he is a double-minded man, unstable in all his ways" (1:5-8). Sometimes our prayers are not answered because we lack faith, and this is often because we resist submitting to God's will. We ask for wisdom but actually desire to do as we wish, and so our sin keeps us from truly asking in faith. Our sin, and doubt is born of sin, hinders us in other requests we direct to God as well.

James explains to us, "You ask and do not receive, because you ask wrongly, to spend it on your passions" (4:3). The requests we make often cannot be answered because they are entwined with selfish desire. This can even extend to our prayers for others, and we can become bitter when those we intercede for experience hardships, or they are not healed of their sicknesses, or they die. We fail to see that death is universal to all people, but for the Christian, it is the beginning of even greater blessings. Still, we regularly take offense with what God has or has not done, but we do so to our own hurt. When we are wrapped up with our own versions of what God's will might entail, we miss the point that Scripture has made plain: "My thoughts are not your thoughts, neither are your ways my ways, declares the Lord. For as the heavens are higher than the earth, so are my ways higher than your ways and my thoughts than your thoughts" (Isaiah 55:8-9).

Therefore, we must not assume all unanswered prayer is due to our sin or disbelief. At times larger and perhaps more mysterious purposes are at stake. Prior to his crucifixion, Jesus prayed to the Heavenly Father, asking, "If possible, let this cup pass from me; nevertheless, not as I will, but as you will" (Matthew 26:39). Indeed, Jesus drank from God's cup of wrath against sin by going to the cross as a perfect sacrifice and substitute for all humanity's transgressions. Consequently, Jesus fulfilled God's purposes, which required that the Heavenly Father not answer his own Son's request to be spared.

The Apostle Paul prayed earnestly for relief from a "thorn in his flesh, a messenger of Satan," and he, too, did not receive the answer he was looking for. While the exact nature of this "thorn" is not known, scholars have speculated that it was perhaps a serious and painful illness or other chronic condition. Whatever it was, Paul realized that the "thorn" was sent to prevent him from "becoming conceited" because of the "surpassing greatness" of revelations he had received. Moreover, God said to him, "My grace is sufficient for you, for my power is made perfect in weakness" (2 Corinthians 12: 7-9).

Similarly, it may be that God withholds a particular answer because giving it would cause us to feel peculiarly blessed or justified, leading to haughtiness and falling away from trust in God himself. This can happen especially when one receives an apparently miraculous answer to prayer, such as healing from a disease or abundant provision for a material need. It is far better to have unanswered prayers while still humbly loving and trusting God, than it is to be arrogantly self-satisfied or presuming upon God's favor.

At times, our works in God may consist of prayer only, and we are instructed that "supplications, prayers, intercessions, and thanksgivings be made for all people, for kings and all who are in high positions, that we may lead a peaceful and quiet life, godly and dignified in every way. This is good, and it is pleasing in the sight of God our Savior, who desires all people to be saved and to come to the knowledge of the truth" (1 Timothy 2: 1-4). We must not discount the value of prayer in and of itself, for "the prayer of a righteous person has great power as it is working. Elijah was a man with a nature like ours, and he prayed fervently that it might not rain, and for three years and six months it did not rain on the earth. Then he prayed again, and heaven gave rain, and the earth bore its fruit" (James 5:16-18). In some situations, we are called to pray, and that is enough.

There are other occasions when prayer is the necessary prerequisite for additional labors. Jesus frequently removed himself from others and spent time communing with his heavenly Father, insuring that his ministry was focused on God's will, not the needs and demands of the people who thronged about him. Out of his own prayer time, Jesus received wisdom about choosing his closest disciples, discerning where they should travel, and determining what works they should undertake (Mark 1:35-39). Likewise, out of our own time spent seeking God and waiting on him, he will move us to take practical steps in serving others by meeting pressing needs, alleviating suffering, giving comfort, or otherwise extending the life and peace of God's kingdom into situations that are bereft of his blessings.

Scriptures for Reflection and Prayer
—

Matthew 26:36-46
1 Timothy 2:1-4
James 5:13-18

XIII | The Kingdom of God

Many Jews of Jesus' day looked for a Savior to come and establish a political kingdom centered in Jerusalem. Indeed, Jesus began his earthly ministry by telling people to "repent, for the kingdom of heaven is at hand," (Matthew 4:17), but it wasn't the kind of reign most were looking for, one in which the oppressive Romans would be thrown down and a Jewish nation would come forth in power. Christ explained that the "kingdom of God is not coming with signs to be observed, nor will they say, 'Look, here it is!' or 'There!' for behold the kingdom of God is in the midst of you" (Luke 17:20-21). Pilate, the Roman official who at the insistence of certain Jews ordered Jesus to be crucified, asked him if he was a king. Jesus acknowledged that he was, but added, "My kingdom is not of this world. If my kingdom were of this world, my servants would have been fighting that I might not be delivered over to the Jews" (John 18:36).

Jesus explained this kingdom in various parables. In one, he compared himself to a man sowing seed, and the seed represented the word of God. Some seed fell on the road and was snatched away. These represented those who do not really hear the word and do not understand it. Other seed fell on rocky soil, which were people who received the word superficially and had "no root" in themselves, so they "fall away when tribulation or persecution arises on account of the word." Some seed also "fell among thorns, and the thorns grew up with it and choked it." These are people "choked by the cares and riches and pleasures of life, and their fruit does not mature." Finally, seed was sown on "good soil" and this represents people who, "hearing the word of God, hold it fast in a good and honest heart and bear fruit with patience" (Luke 8:4-15). From this parable we see that having our portion in this kingdom is a matter of honestly and completely receiving the truth about God and continuing in that revelation.

Because our citizenship is to be in a new and heavenly kingdom, we must view our earthly allegiances as utterly secondary to Christ and his Lordship. He compels us to come unreservedly and completely to him, so much that our own devotion to country and family and even ourselves must pale by comparison. Jesus declared that "if anyone comes to me and does not hate his own father and mother and wife and children and brothers and sisters, yes, and even his own life, he cannot be my disciple" (Luke 14:25-27). Jesus made it clear elsewhere that we are to love others completely and well, but that love could be considered hate in comparison to the love we reserve for Jesus. This love is not just a warm or sentimental feeling, but a consecrated devotion. Because we have seen Christ and his way to be the source and goal of all that is eternally valuable, we can willingly forsake everything for him. Jesus said, "The kingdom of heaven is like treasure hidden in a field, which a man found and covered up. Then in his joy he goes and sells all that he has and buys that field" (Matthew 13:44).

In another parable about the kingdom of God, Jesus represented himself as one sowing seeds again, this time planting wheat in a field, but his enemy sowed weeds among the wheat. Here the field is the world, the wheat represents the "sons of the kingdom," and the weeds are the "sons of the devil." Both weeds and wheat grew together in the same field, but removing the weeds would have uprooted the wheat as well, so he chose to let them grow together until harvest, when the wheat would be gathered into the barn and the weeds would be burned. This indicates that at some time in the future, the true believers will be separated from those without faith, who will be consumed in judgment, and "the righteous will shine like the sun in the kingdom of their Father" (Matthew 13:24-30; 37-43).

In the meantime, however, the kingdom of God coexists among that which is anything but godly. It is only reasonable to conclude that those who belong to the kingdom of God ought to live differently from those around them. Such people are called to be "the light of the world," and Jesus exhorts us: "Let your light shine before others, so that they may see your good works and give glory to your Father who is in heaven" (Matthew 5:14, 16).

Scriptures for Reflection and Prayer

—

Matthew 13:1-50
Luke 8:4-15

XIV | The Church

In his writings, the Apostle Paul refers to the people of Christ as "God's field" (1 Corinthians 3:9), carrying forward the images of God's kingdom found in the parables told by Jesus. Paul elaborates on this idea in his writings and uses other metaphors as well, explaining that believers are a building with Christ as its very foundation (1 Corinthians 3:10-11), and especially that believers are The Body of Christ here on earth (1 Corinthians 12:27). This concept of The Body of Christ resonated with Paul quite profoundly, for he once was a religious zealot going by the name Saul, and he attacked the church, arresting both men and women and putting them in prison (Acts 8:3). Then, a revelation of Christ stopped him in his tracks, and Jesus asked, "Saul, Saul, why are your persecuting me?" (Acts 9:4) At this time Jesus had risen to heaven, but his work and mission continued on by his own Spirit working through his people, so Saul's mistreatment of Christians was much like persecuting Christ himself. Later, this misguided religious man was transformed by Jesus, changed his name to Paul, and became one of the major proponents of the Christian faith, spreading its influence throughout the ancient world.

Granted, many atrocities have been committed in the name of Christ by institutional churches, and individuals corrupting the message and mission of Christ's kingdom have wreaked havoc throughout history. Even at the time when the New Testament was still being written, those who were not true believers "crept in unnoticed" and were "ungodly people, who pervert the grace of our God into sensuality and deny our only Master and Lord, Jesus Christ" (Jude 4). Such people were "fruitless trees in late autumn, twice dead, uprooted; wild waves of the sea, casting up the foam of their own shame; wandering stars, for whom the gloom of utter darkness has been reserved forever" (Jude 12-13). These were "grumblers, malcontents, following their own sinful desires...loud-mouthed boasters showing favoritism to gain an advantage" (Jude 16). Ever since the beginnings of the church, "worldly people, devoid of the Spirit" have created tensions and divisions among the people of God and hindered the work of the kingdom (Jude 19).

It seems that even in the church, which is the visible kingdom of God on earth, the parable of the wheat and the weeds holds true: good and evil will coexist because of God's mercy in withholding judgment, at least for now. Despite this, however, God always "knows those who are his," and while there have been many who have shown themselves to be dishonorable, there have always been those who were "set apart as holy, useful to the master...and ready for every good work." These were the ones who heeded the Spirit, who called them to "flee youthful passions and pursue righteousness, faith, love, and peace, along with those who call on the Lord from a pure heart" (2 Timothy 2:19-22). In many times and in many places, the kingdom of God has been demonstrated through the church "in the midst of a crooked and twisted generation" by children of God who have made it their mission to "shine as lights in the world, holding fast to the word of life" (Philippians 2:15-16).

None of us who belong to Christ are solitary believers. Spiritually, we are all part of the universal church, one that crosses not only denominational lines, but also ones of race, creed, nationality, and culture. Sharing a life in the Spirit together, believers gather in homes, open spaces, public buildings, and structures we mistakenly call churches, for the church is never a physical building. The true church has always been the people of God gathered around the risen Christ in the Spirit of God, not a building or organization.

People sometimes profess to love Christ, but refuse to be part of his church, claiming that religious gatherings are full of hypocrites, busybodies, and greedy opportunists. Such a judgmental and haughty attitude is not fitting for one who claims to follow Christ. If Jesus put aside the privileges of his divinity and physically came into the world to save sinners, and if he still dwells by his Spirit among the believers in his church, how can one who calls on his name be so proud, aloof, and self-centered?

As believers we must allow God to lead us in such a way that we become immersed in the practical reality of his kingdom, a viable and visible expression of the church in a particular place. God himself is behind this great work, and as we submit to his will, he "arranges the members in the body" (1 Corinthians 12:18). Each person has a different function, and "having gifts that differ according to the grace given to us, let us use them: if prophecy, in proportion to our faith, if service, in our serving; the one who teaches, in his teaching; the one who exhorts, in his exhortation; the one who contributes, in generosity; the one who leads, with zeal, the one who does acts of mercy, with cheerfulness" (Romans 12: 6-8). Through all of our actions, there is the possibility of expressing the life of Christ here on the earth because Jesus "gave himself for us to redeem us from all lawlessness and to purify for himself a people for his own possession who are zealous for good works" (Titus 2:14).

Only in the context of Christian community do we completely demonstrate the qualities of Christian love, but these opportunities are missed when Christians in the church behave like unbelievers. Those calling on the name of Christ must learn to "do nothing from rivalry or conceit, but in humility count others more significant than yourselves. Let each of you look not only to his interests, but also to the interests of others" (Philippians 2:3-4). We must be people of grace, "bearing with one another and, if one has a complaint against another, forgiving each other; as the Lord has forgiven you, so you must forgive. And above all these put on love, which binds everything together in perfect harmony" (Colossians 3:13-14).

Jesus said that the world "will know that you are my disciples, if you have love for one another" (John 13:35). In the details of our lives and relationships, we must demonstrate the love of Christ to a world starved for his affections.

Scriptures for Reflection and Prayer

—

Romans 12:1-21
1 Corinthians 3:5-17
1 Corinthians 12:12-31
1 Peter 2: 1-12

XV | In the World but Not of It

Jesus said of his disciples, "They are not of the world, just as I am not of the world" (John 17: 16). By this he meant that even though his followers were living in a particular place and time here on earth, their devotions and affections were focused on the kingdom of heaven. The Apostle John commands us not to love "the things in the world," which include "the desires of the flesh and the desires of the eyes and pride in possessions," for "the world is passing away, along with its desires, but whoever does the will of God abides forever" (1 John 2:15-17).

Here we see that the real issue is actually doing the will of God, not just rejecting worldly goals and pleasures. Contrary to what far too many think, the will of God is not about living lives of isolation or asceticism, nor is it discovering some grandiose mission. Instead, it is actively and reverently honoring our Lord in the details of our daily lives: "See to it that no one repays evil for evil, but always seek to do good to one another and to everyone. Rejoice always, pray without ceasing, give thanks in all circumstances; for this is the will of God in Christ Jesus for you" (1 Thessalonians 5:15-18).

In this world, people find their identity in their professions, positions, physical appearances, and possessions, and they pursue happiness by seeking after their own desires. This ought not to be so for believers because "our lives are hid with Christ in God" (Col 3:1-5), and we only discover our true identity in him. Because of this, the poorer disciple should "boast in his exaltation" in Christ, and the one who is wealthy should be humble, realizing that "like a flower of the grass he will pass away" (James 1:9-10). Because of this eternal perspective, the "rich in this present age" are encouraged "not to be haughty, nor to set their hopes on the uncertainty of riches, but on God, who richly provides us with everything to enjoy. They are to do good, to be rich in good works, to be generous and ready to share...so that they may take hold of that which is truly life" (1Timothy 6:17-19).

Examples of such humility and generosity of spirit are far too rare, even in the church itself, but this has been a problem from the beginning and has only become worse, for "in the last days" people will be "lovers of money, proud, arrogant, abusive...swollen with conceit, lovers of pleasure rather than lovers of God, having the appearance of godliness, but denying its power" (2 Timothy 3:1-5). The Apostle Paul addresses this when he explains that some teachers proclaim "godliness is a means of great gain," as if believing in Christ entitles us to great wealth. He concedes that "there is great gain in godliness with contentment" (I Timothy 6:5-6), and this is the cure for perhaps one of the greatest curses in life--our extreme discontent. Paul explains that we can be happy with only food to eat and clothes to wear, but "those who desire to be rich fall into temptations, into a snare, into many senseless and harmful desires that plunge people into ruin and destruction. For the love of money [not the money itself] is a root of all kinds of evils. It is through this craving that many have wandered away from the faith and pierced themselves with many pangs" (1 Timothy 6:9-10).

In a world filled with selfish ambition and greed, how then should we live? Paul runs counter to prevailing attitudes by declaring that we "have been taught by God to love one another" and "to aspire to live quietly, and to mind your own affairs, and to work... so that you may walk properly before outsiders and be dependent on no one" (1 Thessalonians 4:9-12) In all our pursuits and activities in this life, we should demonstrate our godliness and contentment, and "in our hearts honor Christ the Lord as holy," being ready to explain "the reason for the hope within you; yet do it with gentleness and respect" (1 Peter 3:15).

Granted, we live in a material world and have need of material things, but Jesus taught us, "Your heavenly Father knows that you need these things, but seek first the kingdom of God and his righteousness, and all these things will be added to you" (Matthew 6:33). There is much to enjoy in this life, yet we must guard ourselves against idolatry and our innate tendency to value the gifts of God above the Giver himself. Consequently, we are free to enjoy the good things life has to offer in their proper place: food without gluttony, sex within marriage, and personal ownership without greed. The blessings we can enjoy are lavish and boundless because of God's mercies toward us.

Even when we are so blessed, however, we must exercise godly restraint, and in all our experiences in this earthly life we should recognize that this world is not our true home. "Let those who have wives live as though they had none, and those who mourn as though they were not mourning, and those who rejoice as though they were not rejoicing, and those who buy as though they had no goods, and those who deal with the world as though they had no dealings with it. For the present form of this world is passing away" (1 Corinthians 7:29-31). In all of these admonitions, the Apostle Paul is not encouraging us to ignore our spouses, and he is not telling us to never mourn, rejoice, or purchase merchandise. Instead, we must place Christ above all else because "the things that are seen are transient, but the things that are unseen are eternal" (2 Corinthians 4:18).

In this world a common desire is to be the center of attention, to be the one with power and prestige. We take pride in our appearances and our accomplishments and our positions of power, but Christ confronted this attitude when he said it was not to be this way with his followers: "You know that the rulers of the Gentiles lord it over them and their great ones exercise authority over them. It shall not be so among you. But whoever would be great among you must be your servant, and whoever would be first among you must be your slave, even as the Son of Man came not to be served but to serve, and to give his life as a ransom for many" (Matthew 20: 25-28).

This God-given attitude strikes at the core of worldliness and sin, which is an exaltation of our individual selves over others and even over God. Ironically, some within the church itself manifest attitudes of self-exaltation while teaching and preaching and promoting their causes in the guise of serving God. Instead, when we have done as Christ has truly commanded us to do, we should divert any glory away from ourselves and toward God, declaring, "We are unworthy servants; we have only done what was our duty" (Matthew 17:10).

Pride is the hallmark of worldliness, but we are called to be humble. Even in our refutation of worldliness, though, we must not become arrogant. Instead, we are to be "submissive to rulers and authorities, to be obedient, to be ready for every good work, to speak evil of no one, to avoid quarreling, to be gentle and to show perfect courtesy toward all people. For we ourselves were once foolish, disobedient, led astray, slaves to various passions and pleasures, passing our days in malice and envy, hated by others and hating one another. But when the goodness and loving kindness of God our Savior appeared, he saved us, not because of works done by us in righteousness, but according to his own mercy, by the washing of regeneration and renewal of the Holy Spirit, whom he poured out on us richly through Jesus Christ our Savior" (Titus 3:1-7).

Scriptures for Reflection and Prayer

—

John 17:1-26
1 Corinthians 7:1-9; 17-35
Colossians 3:1-17
1 Timothy 6:3-19
2 Timothy 3:1-5
Titus 2:11-3:11

XVI | Temptation and Sin: Shipwreck of Faith or Victory over the World

The temptations of this world are ever present, so we find ourselves continually resisting sin, both around us and within our very selves. Consequently we must renounce our allegiances to this world, seeing ourselves as "sojourners and exiles" who "abstain from the passions of the flesh, which wage war against your soul." In doing so, we establish the kingdom of God in our hearts, lives, and behaviors so that others may witness the truth and glorify God along with us (I Peter 2:11-12).

As we purpose to live our lives in relationship with God through the Spirit, at times we will literally be at odds with ourselves. The desires of the lower nature oppose those of the Spirit, so that we may not do what we want to do, but we who are led by the Spirit can put down these desires and demonstrate holiness and self-control. Temptation itself is not sin, and God tempts none of us, "but each person is tempted when he is lured and enticed by his own desire. Then desire when it has conceived gives birth to sin, and sin when it is fully grown brings forth death" (James 1:14-15).

Like the Apostle Paul, we find ourselves conflicted, on the one hand wanting to do right, and on the other hand desiring to do the opposite, but as we focus our minds on the Spirit, we can find victory. Those who live according to the Spirit center their minds on the things of the Spirit because "the mind set on the flesh is death, but the mind set on the Spirit is life and peace" (Romans 8:6). We live like God's enemies when focused on our sinful desires and find ourselves actually unable to obey his holy laws, but when we set our minds on the Spirit of Christ within us, we can be alive to righteousness (Romans 8: 7-10).

Our own legalistic tendencies will sever us from the grace found in Christ, and we cannot assume that keeping God's commandments will gain us his favor. As we have received Christ by faith, so we must continue in faith. In Galatians 3:2-3, Paul asked a group of Christians, "Did you receive the Spirit by works of the law or by hearing with faith? Are you so foolish? Having begun by the Spirit, are you now being perfected by the flesh?" The answer, of course, is that by attempting to obey rules and laws we will not make progress in the way of godliness, but we will advance with "faith working through love" (Galatians 5:4-6).

"Therefore, as you received Christ Jesus the Lord, so walk in him, rooted and built up in him and established in the faith" (Colossians 2:6). In other words, we are to continually surrender ourselves to him, turning from sin and clinging to Christ and trusting in the redeeming work he accomplished for us on the cross, just as when we first began. In receiving his mercies, we also have the power and desire for right living. It is important to draw near to God, lest we "be hardened by the deceitfulness of sin" (Hebrews 3:13). Because all sin is violation of love, our transgressions defile our consciences. A lack of sensitivity to sin or the guilt that wrongdoing brings damages our consciences, and because of this "some have made shipwreck of their faith" (1 Timothy 1:19).

Our faith is really what is at stake, and the devil is not so much concerned with our sin as he is with our faith, for faith is the cord that binds us to our Creator in loving relationship. His goal is to sever that bond. Through enticing us to commit acts of blatant sin, our free rapport based on faith is threatened, because "whatever does not proceed from faith is sin" (Romans 14:23), and it is not possible to live in faith and live in sin at the same time. The devil also brings discouragement by reminding us of our failures, for he is "the accuser" of believers everywhere (Revelation 12:12), and in our guilt, we shy away from God instead of rejoicing in his lavish grace. By this grace, "submit yourselves therefore to God. Resist the devil and he will flee from you," for he cannot stand in the presence of God's light, and we are in that light as we are restored to fellowship with him because of what he has done for us in Christ (James 5:6-10).

Scriptures for Reflection and Prayer

—

Romans 6:12-23
Galatians 5:16-24
I Peter 5:6-11

XVII | Remaining in the Light of God

We must be careful to focus on the revelation of God in his Scripture and the illumination God gives us by his own Spirit. Our own thinking can deceive us, and the Apostle Paul made it clear that he was "afraid...your thoughts will be led astray from a sincere and pure devotion to Christ" (2 Corinthians 11:3). In a very real sense, we must wage a mental battle against the influences of the world around us, and even against Satan himself, to prevent having our minds warped and rendered ineffective for devotion to Christ and his kingdom. We are called to "destroy arguments and every lofty opinion raised against the knowledge of God, and take every thought captive to obey Christ" (2 Corinthians 10:5). In our thinking we are not to be simple-minded, but we must realize that there is simplicity of devotion to Christ that has little to do with intellect or haughty and high-minded reason.

Unlike nonbelievers who "walk in the futility of their minds...darkened in their understanding and alienated from the life of God...due to their hardness of heart" (Ephesians 4:17-18), we must turn our backs on our old ways of thinking and "be renewed in the spirit of our minds and put on the new self, created in the likeness of God in true righteousness and holiness" (Ephesians 4:23-24).

What we are called by God to do is not so much adopting new thoughts as it is recognizing that "to set our minds on the Spirit is life and peace" (Romans 8:6), and with this very same Spirit who is God himself, we have a new way of life. When our minds dwell on the needs and pleasures and attitudes of this world, we find ourselves thwarting God and his purposes. Fortunately, we are released from fear and anxiety when we set our minds on the Spirit he has given us and return to the sweet simplicity in which we cry out to God as our own Father, and "the Spirit himself bears witness with our spirit that we are children of God" (Romans 8:16).

As children of God abiding in his love, we are free from the curse of sin and "try to discern what is pleasing to the Lord," rejecting the darkness within and around us so that we see clearly what is good and what is evil (Ephesians 5:9-10). Like children of God, we invariably seek and do what is right and truly love others because "no one born of God makes a practice of sinning" (1 John 3:9), and we can know that we are truly born of him because "we know that he abides in us, by the Spirit he has given us" (1 John 3:24).

Despite the great gift of God's own Spirit within us, we are still far too human, and while we may not seek out sin and make a practice of doing those things that displease our Lord, "we all stumble in many ways" (James 3:2). Walking in the light of Christ illuminates the sin in ourselves and our deeds, but we need not despair, nor do we go back to our former ways of thinking and acting, making excuses for our behavior, explaining away the damages wrought by our transgressions, or lying to ourselves and others by denying that we have done any wrong at all. As is fitting for the people of God, we can know that "if we say we have no sin, we deceive ourselves, and the truth is not in us. If we confess our sins, he is faithful and just to forgive us our sins and to release us from all unrighteousness" (1 John 1:8-9).

This forgiveness we must receive humbly and reverently, with sincere thankfulness, for we are offered no easy pardon when released from the penalty of our transgressions. It is the blood of Christ himself making it possible to continue on in his love and holiness, instead of turning back in denial, doubt, and despair.

Scriptures for Reflection and Prayer
—
Romans 7:21-8:17
Ephesians 4:17-5:21
1 John 1:5-2:6
1 John 3:1-24

XVIII | Trials, Persecution, and Suffering

Besides the internal struggles we have with our own temptations and sins, external trials assail us in varying degrees. The pressures of life turn in upon us, squelching our life and peace, and we worry about our needs, whims, and seemingly endless responsibilities. Consequently, our spiritual selves atrophy and become dormant. The Scriptures declare a better way, exhorting us to "not be anxious for anything, but in everything by prayer and supplication with thanksgiving let your requests be known to God, and the peace of God, which surpasses all understanding, will guard your hearts and minds in Christ Jesus" (Philippians 4:6-7).

As we again focus our attentions on the Lord in prayer, we find much to be thankful for, and at times it is simply this gratefulness that brings healing to our souls. At other times, our requests for various things will be granted, just as we've asked. More than likely, however, as we turn to the Lord, we find that he alone is enough for us, and while our circumstances may not have changed one iota, our souls are sustained with a peace that goes beyond what we can think or imagine.

The world we live in may do more than simply exert pressure upon our souls. Those who dwell in it often come against us, simply because our Gospel of reconciliation with God cuts to the heart of selfishness and greed, and it challenges the power structures of this present world. This drives some to speak evil against the people of God and propels others to anger and even violence toward us and what we believe. We should not be surprised at such persecution, for "all who desire to live a godly life in Christ Jesus will be persecuted, while evil people and impostors will go on from bad to worse, deceiving and being deceived" (2 Timothy 3:12-13).

Jesus likened his own disciples to "sheep in the midst of wolves" and warned them that even "members of their own households" could become enemies because of their faith in him (Matthew 10:16, 36). Of course, a person who claims to be a Christian might endure persecution, not because of righteousness, but because he or she is acting in a manner unbecoming of the Gospel. Christians far too often are arrogant, dogmatic, and misguided, and they meddle in matters that are none of their business. If, however, any of us is suffering for truly living like a Christian, "let him not be ashamed, but let him glorify God in that name" (1 Peter 4:16). In the midst of such suffering, "We rejoice in the hope of the glory of God. More than that, we rejoice in our sufferings, knowing that suffering produces endurance, and endurance produces character, and character produces hope, and hope does not put us to shame because God's love has been poured into our hearts through the Holy Spirit who has been given to us" (Romans 5:2-5). Above all else, we can take comfort in knowing that "the sufferings of this present time are not worth comparing with the glory that is to be revealed in us" (Romans 8:18).

But now we do not see that full glory, for even if we maintain peace in our inner selves and are fortunate enough not to suffer persecution, we all inhabit bodies that are prone to sickness and pain, and we all eventually die. Even the Apostle Paul was "so utterly burdened" that he "despaired of life itself" and felt he had received "the sentence of death." But Paul recognized that these trials were there to make him trust not in himself, but in "God who raises the dead" (2 Corinthians 1:8-9), for while "our outer self is wasting away, our inner self is being renewed day by day" (2 Corinthians 4:16).

Scriptures for Reflection and Prayer
—
Matthew 10:16-39
Romans 8:18-39
2 Corinthians 4:7-18
1 Peter 2:13-25
1 Peter 4:12-19

XIX | The End of Death and Fulfillment of God's Kingdom

Even though the Apostle Paul may have been discouraged by his bodily trials, they did not overcome him, and he had no fear of death because he understood "to live is Christ and to die is gain" (Philippians 1:21). Our bodies may be wasting away, but they are simply part of a physical order that is inevitably deteriorating. All that we can see is temporary, and the eternal remains invisible, glimpsed by faith through the Spirit. Eventually, those who believe will have eternal, heavenly bodies, and the one "who has prepared us for this very thing is God, who gives us his Spirit as a guarantee" (2 Corinthians 5:5). In the meantime, this same Spirit reminds us of that which is eternal and makes a relationship with God himself a reality at the present time. As Jesus said, "This is eternal life, that they know you the only true God, and Jesus Christ whom you have sent" (John 17:3). In a sense, heaven has already begun for the believer, even on this side of death.

While we presently have eternal life and behold Jesus by faith, our lives are still nonetheless incomplete, "for now we see in a mirror dimly, but then face to face. Now I know in part; then I shall know fully, even as I have been fully known" (1 Corinthians 13:12) This fulfillment has many ramifications, not just for Christians, but for the entire created order, because "creation itself will be set free from its bondage to corruption and obtain the freedom of the glory of the children of God. For we know that the whole creation has been groaning together in the pains of childbirth until now. And not only the creation, but we ourselves, who have the first fruits of the Spirit, groan inwardly as we wait eagerly for adoption as sons, the redemption of our bodies" (Romans 8:21-23).

Eventually, we will inherit eternal bodies, and a new heaven and earth will be made manifest, in which righteousness dwells and all wickedness has been eradicated. This will take place after Jesus returns from heaven with those who have already died in faith, and the believers who are still alive will be "caught up with him to be with him forever" (2 Thessalonians 4-5).

After Christ ascended to heaven, some assumed that he would return quickly, and since that time many have speculated as to dates and times for his second coming, even though Jesus made it plain that "no man knows the day or the hour" (Mark 13:32). Many have come claiming to be him, but Jesus warned us, "If anyone says to you, 'Look, here is the Christ!' or 'There he is!' do not believe it. For false christs and false prophets will arise and perform great signs and wonders, so as to lead astray, if possible, even the elect... So, if they say to you, 'Look, he is in the wilderness,' do not go out. If they say, 'Look, he is in the inner rooms,' do not believe it. For as the lightning comes from the east and shines as far as the west, so will be the coming of the Son of Man" (Matthew 24:23-27).

When Christ returns everyone will know it, for he will not be coming as he did the first time, to save sinners and draw them to himself in redemption. Instead, he will come in judgment, putting an end to all wickedness and sending forth his angels to "gather out of his kingdom all causes of sin and all law-breakers, and throw them into the fiery furnace. In that place there will be weeping and gnashing of teeth. Then the righteous will shine like the sun in the kingdom of their Father" (Matthew 13:41-43).

Thus, all evil will be removed, and God's kingdom will be fully established in a new heaven and new earth where God will dwell among his people, unhindered by sin and living in peace and joy. On the other hand, those who have not submitted to Christ's lordship and salvation will be eternally separated from God and his blessed new order. Consequently, Christ's apparent slowness in returning is above all else due to God's kindness and mercy, for "with the Lord one day is as a thousand years, and a thousand years as one day. The Lord is not slow to fulfill his promises as some count slowness, but is patient toward you, not wishing that any should perish, but that all should reach repentance" (2 Peter 3 8-9). We must "watch" ourselves so that our hearts are not "weighed down with dissipations and drunkenness and cares of this life, and that day come upon us suddenly like a trap" (Luke 21:34).

Likewise, believers must glorify God in all we do because we will appear before the "judgment seat of Christ, so that each one may receive what is due, whether good or evil" (2 Corinthians 5:7-10). There we will be rewarded for what we have done in our bodies, or we will suffer great loss, having squandered our gifts from the Lord. Those who have trusted Christ, however, will live forever with him due to the mercies we have found in him, even if our works and rewards may be consumed in the flames of judgment (1 Corinthians 3:10-15).

Faithful believers should not be discouraged, for "we are God's children now, and what we will be has not yet appeared; but we know that when he appears we shall be like him, because we shall see him as he is. And everyone who thus hopes in him purifies himself as he is pure" (1 John 3:2-3). This is the essence of true life: fellowshipping with God in Christ by the Spirit and allowing the kingdom of God to be a progressively expanding reality in our hearts and minds and lives. Until the time we die or meet Jesus at his return, those who believe must—in our own small but eternally significant ways—demonstrate this kingdom before others, so they might also believe and glorify God.

Scriptures for Reflection and Prayer
—

1 Corinthians 15:12-28; 35-58
2 Corinthians 5:1-10
2 Thessalonians 1:5-2:12
2 Peter 3:1-13
Revelation 20:11-21:8

Appendix: Discussion Questions

Individual chapters of this book lend themselves to further study and discussion. The following questions are suggested "starters" for home groups, Bible studies, and other gatherings. Of course, more than one chapter could be discussed; let the dynamics of the group and the leading of the Holy Spirit determine how to direct your meetings.

- Which idea in this chapter made the biggest impression on you? Why?

- Is there something in this chapter that surprised you? If so, how were you surprised?

- Are there ideas in this chapter that are different from those we tend to hear today? If so, what are they? What should our attitude be toward these concepts?

- How do these ideas from the Bible apply today?

- Are there any specific Bible verses referenced in this chapter that confused you or gave you particular insights? If so, what are they?

- What do you think is the main idea of this chapter?

- Based on what you have read in this chapter, what changes do you think God desires for you to make in your opinions, attitudes, and behaviors?

Made in the USA
Charleston, SC
13 July 2014